16th Conference of the European Chapter of the Association for Computational Linguistics (EACL 2021)

Tutorial Abstracts

Held online due to COVID-19

Kiev, Ukraine
21 – 23 April 2021

ISBN: 978-1-7138-2917-1

Printed from e-media with permission by:

Curran Associates, Inc.
57 Morehouse Lane
Red Hook, NY 12571

CURRAN ASSOCIATES INC. proceedings .com

Some format issues inherent in the e-media version may also appear in this print version.

Printed with permission by Curran Associates, Inc. (2021)

For permission requests, please contact the Association for Computational Linguistics at the address below.

Association for Computational Linguistics
209 N. Eighth Street
Stroudsburg, Pennsylvania 18360

Phone: 1-570-476-8006
Fax: 1-570-476-0860

acl@aclweb.org

Additional copies of this publication are available from:

Curran Associates, Inc.
57 Morehouse Lane
Red Hook, NY 12571 USA
Phone: 845-758-0400
Fax: 845-758-2633
Email: curran@proceedings.com
Web: www.proceedings.com

EACL 2021

The 16th Conference of the European Chapter of the Association for Computational Linguistics

Tutorial Abstracts

April 19 - 20, 2021

Message from the Tutorial Chairs

Welcome to the Tutorials Session of EACL 2021.

The 2021 EACL tutorials session includes courses on a variety of topics reflecting recent advances in Natural Language Processing methods and applications, especially selected to give conference attendees comprehensive overviews ranging from introductory to cutting-edge topics targeted to wide audience and presented by experts from academia and industry.

This year, continuing the tradition of the past few years, the call, submission, reviewing and selection of tutorials were coordinated jointly for multiple conferences: EACL, NAACL-HLT, ACL-IJCNLP and EMNLP. The reviewing committee consisted of 19 members, namely the tutorial chairs of the above-mentioned conferences (Isabelle Augenstein and Ivan Habernal for EACL, Greg Kondrak and Kalina Bontcheva for NAACL-HLT, David Chiang and Min Zhang for ACL-IJCNLP and Jing Jiang and Ivan Vulić for EMNLP). Each proposal received two reviews, and was evaluated for clarity, preparedness, novelty, timeliness, instructors' experience, likely audience, open access to the teaching materials, diversity (multilingualism, gender, age and geolocation) and the compatibility of preferred venues. Out of the 34 tutorial submissions received, 5 were selected for presentation at EACL.

We solicited two types of tutorials, including cutting-edge and introductory themes. Out of the 5 tutorials accepted to EACL, 3 are introductory and 2 are cutting-edge tutorials, all reflecting current topics of interest to the community. The introductory tutorials offer overviews of unsupervised parsing, learning from multiple annotators, and on peer review of NLP research. The cutting-edge tutorials present research on methods for speech translation and unsupervised neural machine translation.

We would like to thank the NAACL-HLT, ACL-IJCNLP and EMNLP tutorial chairs, along with the members of the reviewing committee, who all collaborated to ensure a smooth selection process. Our thanks to the conference organisers for an effective and smooth collaboration, and in particular to the general chair Paola Merlo, the program chairs Jorg Tiedemann and Reut Tsarfaty, the publication chairs Valerio Basile and Tommaso Caselli, and the local chairs Viktoria Kolomiets, Dmytro Lider, Iryna Kotkalova, Oleksii Molchanovskyi and Oles Dobosevych. Finally, our thanks goes to the tutorial authors for sending in their tutorial proposals, and for their flexibility and collaboration in a period of adaption to virtual conferences.

We hope you enjoy the tutorials.

EACL 2021 Tutorial Co-chairs
Isabelle Augenstein
Ivan Habernal

Organizing Committee

General Chair

Paola Merlo, University of Geneva

Program Chairs

Jorg Tiedemann, University of Helsinki
Reut Tsarfaty, Bar Ilan University

Tutorial Chairs

Isabelle Augenstein, University of Copenhagen
Ivan Habernal, Technische Universitaet Darmstadt

Table of Contents

Conference Program

Unsupervised Natural Language Parsing (Introductory Tutorial)
Kewei Tu, Yong Jiang, Wenjuan Han and Yanpeng Zhao

Aggregating and Learning from Multiple Annotators
Silviu Paun and Edwin Simpson

Tutorial Proposal: End-to-End Speech Translation
Jan Niehues, Elizabeth Salesky, Marco Turchi and Matteo Negri

Reviewing Natural Language Processing Research
Kevin Cohen, Karën Fort, Margot Mieskes, Aurélie Névéol and Anna Rogers

Advances and Challenges in Unsupervised Neural Machine Translation
Rui Wang and Hai Zhao

Unsupervised Natural Language Parsing (Introductory Tutorial)

Kewei Tu[1], **Yong Jiang**[2], **Wenjuan Han**[3], **Yanpeng Zhao**[4]
[1]School of Information Science and Technology, ShanghaiTech University
[2]Alibaba DAMO Academy, Alibaba Group
[3]School of Computing, National University of Singapore, Singapore
[4]ILCC, University of Edinburgh
tukw@shanghaitech.edu.cn
yongjiang.jy@alibaba-inc.com
dcshanw@nus.edu.sg
yanp.zhao@ed.ac.uk

1 Introduction

Syntactic parsing is an important task in natural language processing that aims to uncover the syntactic structure (e.g., a constituent or dependency tree) of an input sentence. Such syntactic structures have been found useful in downstream tasks such as semantic parsing, relation extraction, and machine translation.

Supervised learning is the main technique used to automatically learn a syntactic parser from data. It requires the training sentences to be manually annotated with their correct parse trees. A major challenge faced by supervised parsing is that syntactically annotated sentences are not always available for a target language or domain and building a high-quality annotated corpus is very expensive and time-consuming.

A radical solution to this challenge is *unsupervised parsing*, sometimes also called *grammar induction*, which learns a parser from training sentences without parse tree annotations. Unsupervised parsing can also serve as the basis for semi-supervised and transfer learning of syntactic parsers when there exist both unannotated sentences and (in-domain or out-of-domain) annotated sentences. In addition, the research of unsupervised parsing is deemed interesting in the field of machine learning because it is a representative task of unsupervised structured prediction, and in the field of cognitive science because it inspires and verifies cognitive research of human language acquisition.

The research on unsupervised parsing has a long history, dating back to theoretical studies in 1960s (Gold, 1967) and algorithmic and empirical studies in 1970s (Baker, 1979). Although deemed an interesting topic by the NLP community, unsupervised parsing had received much less attention than supervised parsing over the past few decades.

More recently, however, there has been a resurgence of interest in unsupervised parsing, with more than ten papers on unsupervised parsing published in top NLP and AI venues over the past two years, including a best paper at ICLR 2019 (Shen et al., 2019), a best paper nominee at ACL 2019 (Shi et al., 2019), and a best paper nominee at EMNLP 2020 (Zhao and Titov, 2020). This renewed interest in unsupervised parsing can be attributed to the combination of two recent trends. First, there is a general trend in deep learning towards unsupervised training or pre-training. Second, there is an emerging trend in the NLP community towards finding or modeling linguistic structures in neural models. The research on unsupervised parsing fits these two trends perfectly.

Because of the renewed attention on unsupervised parsing and its relevance to the recent trends in the NLP community, we believe a tutorial on unsupervised parsing can be timely and beneficial to many *ACL conference attendees. The tutorial will introduce to the general audience what unsupervised parsing does and how it can be useful for and beyond syntactic parsing. It will then provide a systematic overview of major classes of approaches to unsupervised parsing, namely generative and discriminative approaches, and analyze their relative strengths and weaknesses. It will cover both decade-old statistical approaches and more recent neural approaches to give the audience a sense of the historical and recent development of the field. We also plan to discuss emerging research topics such as BERT-based approaches and visually grounded learning.

We expect that by taking this tutorial, one can not only obtain a deep understanding of the literature and methodology of unsupervised parsing and become well prepared for his own research into unsupervised parsing, but may also get inspirations from the ideas and techniques of unsupervised pars-

Proceedings of EACL: Tutorials, pages 1–5
April 19 - 20, 2021.

ing and apply or extend them to other NLP tasks that can potentially benefit from implicitly learned linguistic structures.

2 Overview

This will be a three-hour tutorial divided into five parts.

In the first part, we will introduce the unsupervised parsing task. We will start with the problem definition and discuss the motivations and applications of unsupervised parsing. For example, we will show that unsupervised parsing approaches can be extended for semi-supervised parsing (Jia et al., 2020) and cross-lingual syntactic transfer (He et al., 2019), and we will also show applications of unsupervised parsing approaches beyond syntactic parsing (e.g., in computer vision (Tu et al., 2013)). We will then discuss how to evaluate unsupervised parsing, including the evaluation metrics and typical experimental setups. We will promote standardized setups to enable meaningful empirical comparison between approaches (Li et al., 2020). Finally, we will give an overview of unsupervised parsing approaches to be discussed in the rest of the tutorial.

In the second and third parts, we will introduce in detail two major classes of approaches to unsupervised parsing, generative and discriminative approaches, and discuss their pros and cons.

The second part will cover generative approaches, which model the joint probability of the sentence and the corresponding parse tree. Most of the existing generative approaches are based on generative grammars, in particular context-free grammars and dependency models with valence (Klein and Manning, 2004). There are also featurized and neural extensions of generative grammars, such as Berg-Kirkpatrick et al. (2010); Jiang et al. (2016). We will divide our discussion of learning generative grammars into two parts: structure learning and parameter learning. Structure learning concerns finding the optimal set of grammar rules. We will introduce both probabilistic methods such as Stolcke and Omohundro (1994) and heuristic methods such as Clark (2007). Parameter learning concerns learning the probabilities or weights of a pre-specified set of grammar rules. We will discuss a variety of priors and regularizations designed to improve parameter learning, such as Cohen and Smith (2010), Tu and Honavar (2012), Noji et al. (2016), and (Jin et al., 2018). We will also discuss parameter learning algorithms such as expectation-maximization (Baker, 1979; Spitkovsky et al., 2010b), MCMC (Johnson et al., 2007) and curriculum learning (Spitkovsky et al., 2010a). After introducing approaches based on generative grammars, we will discuss recent approaches that are instead based on neural language models (Shen et al., 2018, 2019).

The third part will cover discriminative approaches, which model the conditional probability or score of the parse tree given the sentence. We will first introduce autoencoder approaches such as Cai et al. (2017), which contain an encoder that maps the sentence to an intermediate representation (such as a parse tree) and a decoder that tries to reconstruct the sentence. Their training objective is typically the reconstruction probability. We will then introduce variational autoencoder approaches such as Kim et al. (2019), which has a similar model structure to autoencoder approaches but uses the evidence lower bound as the training objective. Finally, we will briefly discuss other discriminative approaches such as Grave and Elhadad (2015).

In the fourth part, we will focus on several special topics. First, while most of the previous approaches to unsupervised parsing are unlexicalized, we will discuss the impact of partial and full lexicalization (e.g., the work by Pate and Johnson (2016); Han et al. (2017)). Second, we will discuss whether and how big training data could benefit unsupervised parsing (Han et al., 2017). Third, we will introduce recent attempts to induce syntactic parses from pretrained language models such as BERT (Rosa and Mareček, 2019; Wu et al., 2020). Fourth, we will cover unsupervised multilingual parsing, the task of performing unsupervised parsing jointly on multiple languages (e.g., the work by Berg-Kirkpatrick and Klein (2010); Han et al. (2019)). Fifth, we will introduce visually grounded unsupervised parsing, which tries to improve unsupervised parsing with the help from visual data (Shi et al., 2019). Finally, we will discuss latent tree models trained with feedback from downstream tasks, which are related to unsupervised parsing (Yogatama et al., 2016; Choi et al., 2018).

In the last part, we will summarize the tutorial and discuss potential future research directions of unsupervised parsing.

3 Outline

Part 1. Introduction [20 min]

- Problem definition
- Motivations and applications
- Evaluation
- Overview of approaches

Part 2. Generative Approaches [60 min]

- Overview
- Approaches based on generative grammars
  - Structure learning
  - Parameter learning
- Approaches based on language models

Coffee Break [30 min]

Part 3. Discriminative Approaches [40 min]

- Overview
- Autoencoders
- Variational autoencoders
- Other discriminative approaches

Part 4. Special Topics [50 min]

- Lexicalization
- Big training data
- BERT-based approaches
- Unsupervised multilingual parsing
- Visually grounded unsupervised parsing
- Latent tree models with downstream tasks

Part 5. Summary and Future Directions [10 min]

4 Prerequisites for the Attendees

Linguistics Familiarity with grammars and syntactic parsing.

Machine Learning Basic knowledge about generative vs. discriminative models, unsupervised learning algorithms (such as expectation-maximization), and deep learning.

5 Reading List

Klein and Manning (2004) – An influential generative approach to unsupervised dependency parsing that is the basis for many subsequent papers.

Jiang et al. (2016) – A neural extension of Klein and Manning (2004). One of the first modern neural approaches to unsupervised parsing.

Stolcke and Omohundro (1994) – One of the first structure learning approaches of context-free grammars for unsupervised constituency parsing.

Tu and Honavar (2012) – A parameter learning approach to unsupervised dependency parsing based on unambiguity regularization.

Cai et al. (2017) – An autoencoder approach to unsupervised dependency parsing.

Kim et al. (2019) – A variational autoencoder approach to unsupervised constituency parsing.

6 Presenters

Kewei Tu (ShanghaiTech University)
`http://faculty.sist.shanghaitech.edu.cn/faculty/tukw/`
Kewei Tu is an associate professor with the School of Information Science and Technology at ShanghaiTech University. His research lies in the areas of natural language processing, machine learning, and artificial intelligence in general, with a focus on the representation, learning and application of linguistic structures. He has over 50 publications in NLP and AI conferences and journals including ACL, EMNLP, AAAI, IJCAI, NeurIPS and ICCV. He served as an area chair for the syntax track at EMNLP 2020.

Yong Jiang (Alibaba DAMO Academy)
`http://jiangyong.site`
Yong Jiang is a researcher at Alibaba DAMO Academy, Alibaba Group. He received his Ph.D. degree from the joint program of ShanghaiTech University and University of Chinese Academy of Sciences. He was a visiting student at University of California, Berkeley in 2016. His research interest mainly focuses on machine learning and natural language processing, especially multilingual and unsupervised natural language processing. His research has been published in top-tier conferences and journals including ACL, EMNLP and AAAI.

Wenjuan Han (National University of Singapore)
`http://hanwenjuan.com`
Wenjuan Han is a research fellow at National University of Singapore. She received her Ph.D. degree from the joint program of ShanghaiTech University and University of Chinese Academy of Sciences. She was a visiting student at University of California, Los Angeles in 2019. Her research focuses on natural language understanding, especially unsupervised syntactic parsing. Her research has been published in top-tier *ACL conferences.

Yanpeng Zhao (University of Edinburgh)
`https://zhaoyanpeng.github.io/`
Yanpeng Zhao is a Ph.D. student in the Institute for Language, Cognition and Computation (ILCC) at the University of Edinburgh. His research interests lie in structured prediction and latent variable models with a focus on syntactic parsing and relation induction. His work was nominated for the best paper award at ACL 2018 and received an honorable mention for best paper award at EMNLP 2020.

References

J. K. Baker. 1979. Trainable grammars for speech recognition. In *Speech Communication Papers for the 97th Meeting of the Acoustical Society of America*.

Taylor Berg-Kirkpatrick, Alexandre Bouchard-Côté, John DeNero, and Dan Klein. 2010. Painless unsupervised learning with features. In *NAACL*.

Taylor Berg-Kirkpatrick and Dan Klein. 2010. Phylogenetic grammar induction. In *ACL*.

Jiong Cai, Yong Jiang, and Kewei Tu. 2017. CRF autoencoder for unsupervised dependency parsing. In *EMNLP*.

Jihun Choi, Kang Min Yoo, and Sang-goo Lee. 2018. Unsupervised learning of task-specific tree structures with tree-lstms. *AAAI*.

A. Clark. 2007. Learning deterministic context free grammars: The omphalos competition. *Machine Learning*, 66.

Shay B Cohen and Noah A Smith. 2010. Covariance in unsupervised learning of probabilistic grammars. *The Journal of Machine Learning Research*.

E. Mark Gold. 1967. Language identification in the limit. *Information and Control*, 10(5):447–474.

Edouard Grave and Noémie Elhadad. 2015. A convex and feature-rich discriminative approach to dependency grammar induction. In *ACL-IJCNLP*.

Wenjuan Han, Yong Jiang, and Kewei Tu. 2017. Dependency grammar induction with neural lexicalization and big training data. In *EMNLP*.

Wenjuan Han, Ge Wang, Yong Jiang, and Kewei Tu. 2019. Multilingual grammar induction with continuous language identification. In *EMNLP*.

Junxian He, Zhisong Zhang, Taylor Berg-Kirkpatrick, and Graham Neubig. 2019. Cross-lingual syntactic transfer through unsupervised adaptation of invertible projections. In *Proceedings of the 57th Annual Meeting of the Association for Computational Linguistics*, pages 3211–3223, Florence, Italy. Association for Computational Linguistics.

Zixia Jia, Youmi Ma, Jiong Cai, and Kewei Tu. 2020. Semi-supervised semantic dependency parsing using CRF autoencoders. In *Proceedings of the 58th Annual Meeting of the Association for Computational Linguistics*, pages 6795–6805, Online. Association for Computational Linguistics.

Yong Jiang, Wenjuan Han, and Kewei Tu. 2016. Unsupervised neural dependency parsing. In *EMNLP*.

Lifeng Jin, Finale Doshi-Velez, Timothy Miller, William Schuler, and Lane Schwartz. 2018. Depth-bounding is effective: Improvements and evaluation of unsupervised PCFG induction. In *Proceedings of the 2018 Conference on Empirical Methods in Natural Language Processing*, pages 2721–2731, Brussels, Belgium. Association for Computational Linguistics.

Mark Johnson, Thomas L. Griffiths, and Sharon Goldwater. 2007. Bayesian inference for pcfgs via markov chain monte carlo. In *HLT-NAACL*, pages 139–146.

Yoon Kim, Alexander M Rush, Lei Yu, Adhiguna Kuncoro, Chris Dyer, and Gábor Melis. 2019. Unsupervised recurrent neural network grammars. In *NAACL*.

Dan Klein and Christopher D. Manning. 2004. Corpus-based induction of syntactic structure: Models of dependency and constituency. In *ACL*.

Jun Li, Yifan Cao, Jiong Cai, Yong Jiang, and Kewei Tu. 2020. An empirical comparison of unsupervised constituency parsing methods. In *Proceedings of the 58th Annual Meeting of the Association for Computational Linguistics*, pages 3278–3283, Online. Association for Computational Linguistics.

Hiroshi Noji, Yusuke Miyao, and Mark Johnson. 2016. Using left-corner parsing to encode universal structural constraints in grammar induction. In *EMNLP*.

John K Pate and Mark Johnson. 2016. Grammar induction from (lots of) words alone. In *COLING*.

Rudolf Rosa and David Mareček. 2019. Inducing syntactic trees from bert representations. In *BlackboxNLP*.

Yikang Shen, Zhouhan Lin, Chin wei Huang, and Aaron Courville. 2018. Neural language modeling by jointly learning syntax and lexicon. In *International Conference on Learning Representations*.

Yikang Shen, Shawn Tan, Alessandro Sordoni, and Aaron Courville. 2019. Ordered neurons: Integrating tree structures into recurrent neural networks. In *International Conference on Learning Representations*.

Haoyue Shi, Jiayuan Mao, Kevin Gimpel, and Karen Livescu. 2019. Visually grounded neural syntax acquisition. *arXiv preprint arXiv:1906.02890*.

Valentin I. Spitkovsky, Hiyan Alshawi, and Daniel Jurafsky. 2010a. From Baby Steps to Leapfrog: How "Less is More" in unsupervised dependency parsing. In *NAACL*.

Valentin I Spitkovsky, Hiyan Alshawi, Daniel Jurafsky, and Christopher D Manning. 2010b. Viterbi training improves unsupervised dependency parsing. In *CoNLL*.

Andreas Stolcke and Stephen Omohundro. 1994. Inducing probabilistic grammars by bayesian model merging. In *International Colloquium on Grammatical Inference*.

Kewei Tu and Vasant Honavar. 2012. Unambiguity regularization for unsupervised learning of probabilistic grammars. In *EMNLP-CoNLL*.

Kewei Tu, Maria Pavlovskaia, and Song-Chun Zhu. 2013. Unsupervised structure learning of stochastic and-or grammars. In *Advances in Neural Information Processing Systems 26*, pages 1322–1330.

Zhiyong Wu, Yun Chen, Ben Kao, and Qun Liu. 2020. Perturbed masking: Parameter-free probing for analyzing and interpreting BERT. In *Proceedings of the 58th Annual Meeting of the Association for Computational Linguistics*, pages 4166–4176, Online. Association for Computational Linguistics.

Dani Yogatama, Phil Blunsom, Chris Dyer, Edward Grefenstette, and Wang Ling. 2016. Learning to compose words into sentences with reinforcement learning. In *ICLR*.

Yanpeng Zhao and Ivan Titov. 2020. Visually grounded compound PCFGs. In *Proceedings of the 2020 Conference on Empirical Methods in Natural Language Processing (EMNLP)*, pages 4369–4379, Online. Association for Computational Linguistics.

Aggregating and Learning from Multiple Annotators

https://sites.google.com/view/alma-tutorial

Silviu Paun
Queen Mary University of London
s.paun@qmul.ac.uk

Edwin Simpson
University of Bristol
edwin.simpson@bristol.ac.uk

Abstract

The success of NLP research is founded on high-quality annotated datasets, which are usually obtained from multiple expert annotators or crowd workers. The standard practice to training machine learning models is to first adjudicate the disagreements and then perform the training. To this end, there has been a lot of work on aggregating annotations, particularly for classification tasks. However, many other tasks, particularly in NLP, have unique characteristics not considered by standard models of annotation, e.g., label interdependencies in sequence labelling tasks, unrestricted labels for anaphoric annotation, or preference labels for ranking texts. In recent years, researchers have picked up on this and are covering the gap. A first objective of this tutorial is to connect NLP researchers with state-of-the-art aggregation models for a diverse set of canonical language annotation tasks. There is also a growing body of recent work arguing that following the convention and training with adjudicated labels ignores any uncertainty the labellers had in their classifications, which results in models with poorer generalisation capabilities. Therefore, a second objective of this tutorial is to teach NLP workers how they can augment their (deep) neural models to learn from data with multiple interpretations.

1 Description

The disagreement between annotators stems from ambiguous or subjective annotation tasks as well as annotator errors. Crowdsourcing with non-expert annotators is especially prone to annotation errors, sometimes caused by workers who do not attempt to provide correct annotations (spammers). The traditional resolution to this problem is redundant labeling: collect multiple interpretations from distinct coders, allowing the resource creators to later aggregate these labels. To this end, probabilistic models of annotation have been successfully used to learn the coders' behavior and distill the labels from noise.

The research on models of annotation contains a large body of work spanning multiple decades (from the work on latent structure analysis back in the early 70s), and has been substantially debated over the years at dedicated conferences such as HCOMP and workshops, e.g., from The People's Web Meets NLP (Gurevych and Zesch, 2009), to CrowdML (http://crowdml.cc/), and more recently AnnoNLP (Paun and Hovy, 2019). The plethora of models that had been published even prompted some researchers to ask, challengingly, whether the problem of aggregating crowd labels had been solved (Zheng et al., 2017). As anticipated, there are still unaddressed issues – in particular, the bulk of work has focused on classification tasks, leaving room for innovation in other areas. The NLP field specifically contains a number of tasks with unique characteristics not considered by standard models of annotation. For example, in sequence labeling tasks such as part of speech tagging or named entity recognition, nearby labels have known inter dependencies. In other tasks such as anaphoric annotation for coreference resolution, the coders are asked to provide labels that are not from a fixed set of categories but consist of textual mentions. Another example is pairwise preference labelling, where coders are asked to choose the instance from a pair that most strongly reflects a quality of interest, such as relevance to a topic or convincingness of an argument, with the goal of inferring an overall ranking of text instances. Researchers have observed these gaps in the literature and are addressing them. A key objective of this tutorial is to connect NLP researchers with state-of-the-art aggregation methods suitable for canonical NLP tasks, covering classifications (Yan et al., 2014), sequence labels (Nguyen et al., 2017;

Proceedings of EACL: Tutorials, pages 6–9
April 19 - 20, 2021.

Simpson and Gurevych, 2019), anaphoric interpretations (Paun et al., 2018b) and pairwise preference labels (Simpson and Gurevych, 2020).

Resource creators can use aggregation methods to adjudicate the disagreements inherent in annotated data, but at times, when the resource is to serve as training data to a machine learning model, the noise distillation procedure does not have to be separated and can be integrated into the learning process. In fact, by following the convention and training with adjudicated labels we ignore any of the uncertainty the labellers had in their classifications. Including the coders' disagreements in the learning signal offers the models a richer source of information compared to adjudicated labels: they include not only the consensus, but may also indicate ambiguity, and how the humans make mistakes. This improves the generalisation capability of the models and offers them a more graceful degradation with less ridiculous mistakes (Peterson et al., 2019; Guan et al., 2018). Some of these approaches can also be used for their noise distillation capabilities, as their learning processes also produce aggregated labels that leverage not only coder annotation patterns but also the knowledge of the task accumulated by the model (Cao et al., 2018; Rodrigues and Pereira, 2018; Albarqouni et al., 2016; Chu et al., 2020). Often, this means that fewer redundant labels are required to attain the desired level of accuracy for the aggregated labels. Thus, a second objective of the tutorial is to teach NLP researchers how they can augment their existing (deep) neural architectures to learn from data with disagreements.

1.1 Learning outcomes

We aim to guide NLP practitioners through the emerging body of literature and train them to:

1. Apply aggregation methods and interpret their output predictions;

2. Identify state-of-the-art aggregation methods for canonical NLP tasks: classification, sequence labelling, anaphoric interpretations, and pairwise preferences;

3. Augment a (deep) neural network architecture to learn from data with multiple interpretations.

1.2 Type of tutorial

Introductory. The content will reference and explain well-established work but the focus is on novel, state-of-the-art methods.

2 Outline of Tutorial

Part 1. Motivation and Early Approaches to Annotation Analysis

1. Introduction to the field. Shortcomings of early practices.

2. Modeling the annotation process with a probabilistic model. How to encode our assumptions about the coders, the difficulty of the items, and their interactions. Using hierarchical models to alleviate sparsity.

Part 2. Advanced Models of Annotation

3. Aggregating sequence labels. In such tasks the labels of nearby items have known interdependencies. We discuss probabilistic approaches that model these sequential dependencies both between the ground truth labels and the annotations. We exemplify the utility of the methods on a NER task.

4. Aggregating anaphoric judgements for coreference resolution. For this task the annotation scheme does not use a fixed class space. The judgements here consist of labels assigned to textual mentions that mark when new entities are introduced into the discourse, non refering expressions such as expletives or predicative NPs, and recent antecedents of previously discussed entities. We explain how to apply a probabilistic mention-pair model to aggregate the labels and build coreference chains.

5. Preference labels: why comparisons can be more reliable than ratings or classifications. We show how to reformulate NLP tasks with ambiguous categories or scores as preference learning, giving an example applications related to argument persuasiveness. We introduce probabilistic approaches for aggregating preference judgements to infer a gold standard ranking.

6. Aggregation with Variational Autoencoders. This framework allows us to use neural networks to capture complex non linear relationships between the annotations and the ground truth. By doing so, we avoid having to manually identify and specify these relationships as in standard probabilistic models.

Part 3. Learning with Multiple Annotators

7. Learning with human uncertainty. The standard for training classifiers is to learn from data where each example has a single label. In doing so however any uncertainty the labellers had in their classification is ignored. We discuss here a few approaches to learning from the label distributions produced by the coders, which can improve classifier performance.

8. Humans are noisy. The success of the approaches from the previous point relies on the quality of the target distributions, i.e., whether the collected annotations offer a good representation of the coders' dissent. That may not always be the case, e.g., when their number is too low to get a good proxy for the human uncertainty, or when noise intervenes and skews the distributions. For this purpose we discuss a few training approaches that also capture the accuracy and alleviate the bias of the coders, with an emphasis on neural methods.

Part 4. Practical Session

9. Introduce the audience to an implementation of a probabilistic (Dawid and Skene, 1979) and a neural (Rodrigues and Pereira, 2018) model of annotation. The instructors will provide an example dataset and implementations of the two models then run through a few short exercises that will help the audience to understand and apply the methods to a real NLP task. The exercises will include comparing majority voting with the model of Dawid and Skene (1979) and training a downstream model on adjudicated labels compared to training directly on crowdsourced labels with (Rodrigues and Pereira, 2018). The dataset and code will be provided freely on the tutorial website.

2.1 Audience prerequisites

The audience may benefit from basic knowledge of probability theory, and of neural networks, but all concepts will be introduced from scratch. For the exercises, basic programming skills of Python and familiarity with Keras (in Tensorflow) are useful. The NLP task examples do not require detailed knowledge of the tasks themselves and the course is designed to be accessible for researchers who are new to the field.

2.2 Recommended reading list

Recommendations for part 1:

1. Passonneau and Carpenter (2014)
2. Paun et al. (2018a)

Recommendations for part 2:

3. Simpson et al. (2019)
4. Yin et al. (2017)

Recommendations for part 3:

5. Peterson et al. (2019)
6. Rodrigues and Pereira (2018)

3 Presenters

Silviu Paun, Queen Mary University of London (`s.paun@qmul.ac.uk`).

Silviu (`https://silviupaun.com/`) is a postdoctoral researcher with expertise in label aggregation and training of models on data with disagreements. He is part of the DALI project (`http://dali.eecs.qmul.ac.uk/`), in charge of the analysis of the annotations collected using Phrase Detectives, a GWAP (game with a purpose) developed for gathering labels for coreference resolution, with over 5 million judgements collected. He is regularly involved in machine learning seminars, one of which he organises at Queen Marry University of London, delivering lectures on probabilistic models for NLP applications and parameter estimation techniques.

Edwin Simpson, University of Bristol (`edwin.simpson@bristol.ac.uk`).

Edwin is a lecturer (assistant professor) who is leading new courses on Dialogue and Narrative and Text Analytics at the University of Bristol. During his PhD, he researched probabilistic aggregation methods for crowdsourced data, working with Zooniverse (`https://www.zooniverse.org/`), the world's largest volunteer crowdsourcing effort, and has advised numerous partners in science and industry on crowdsourced data aggregation (e.g., `https://alephinsights.com`). Recently, he led a well-received seminar course and lectures on crowdsourcing and gave tutorials on Bayesian methods at Technische Universität Darmstadt. His research involves developing preference learning techniques for NLP tasks and learning from interactions with end users and crowds.

References

S. Albarqouni, C. Baur, F. Achilles, V. Belagiannis, S. Demirci, and N. Navab. 2016. Aggnet: Deep learning from crowds for mitosis detection in breast cancer histology images. *IEEE Transactions on Medical Imaging*, 35(5):1313–1321.

Peng Cao, Yilun Xu, Yuqing Kong, and Yizhou Wang. 2018. Max-mig: an information theoretic approach for joint learning from crowds. In *International Conference on Learning Representations*.

Zhendong Chu, Jing Ma, and Hongning Wang. 2020. Learning from crowds by modeling common confusions.

Alexander Philip Dawid and Allan M Skene. 1979. Maximum likelihood estimation of observer error-rates using the EM algorithm. *Journal of the Royal Statistical Society: Series C (Applied Statistics)*, 28(1):20–28.

Melody Guan, Varun Gulshan, Andrew Dai, and Geoffrey Hinton. 2018. Who said what: Modeling individual labelers improves classification.

Iryna Gurevych and Torsten Zesch, editors. 2009. *Proceedings of the 2009 Workshop on The People's Web Meets NLP: Collaboratively Constructed Semantic Resources (People's Web)*. Association for Computational Linguistics, Suntec, Singapore.

An Thanh Nguyen, Byron Wallace, Junyi Jessy Li, Ani Nenkova, and Matthew Lease. 2017. Aggregating and predicting sequence labels from crowd annotations. In *Proceedings of the 55th Annual Meeting of the Association for Computational Linguistics (Volume 1: Long Papers)*, pages 299–309, Vancouver, Canada. Association for Computational Linguistics.

Rebecca J. Passonneau and Bob Carpenter. 2014. The benefits of a model of annotation. *Transactions of the Association for Computational Linguistics*, 2:311–326.

Silviu Paun, Bob Carpenter, Jon Chamberlain, Dirk Hovy, Udo Kruschwitz, and Massimo Poesio. 2018a. Comparing bayesian models of annotation. *Transactions of the Association for Computational Linguistics*, 6:571–585.

Silviu Paun, Jon Chamberlain, Udo Kruschwitz, Juntao Yu, and Massimo Poesio. 2018b. A probabilistic annotation model for crowdsourcing coreference. In *Proceedings of the 2018 Conference on Empirical Methods in Natural Language Processing*, pages 1926–1937, Brussels, Belgium. Association for Computational Linguistics.

Silviu Paun and Dirk Hovy, editors. 2019. *Proceedings of the First Workshop on Aggregating and Analysing Crowdsourced Annotations for NLP*. Association for Computational Linguistics, Hong Kong.

Joshua C. Peterson, Ruairidh M. Battleday, Thomas L. Griffiths, and Olga Russakovsky. 2019. Human uncertainty makes classification more robust. In *Proceedings of the IEEE/CVF International Conference on Computer Vision (ICCV)*.

Filipe Rodrigues and Francisco C Pereira. 2018. Deep learning from crowds. In *Thirty-Second AAAI Conference on Artificial Intelligence*.

Edwin Simpson, Erik-Lân Do Dinh, Tristan Miller, and Iryna Gurevych. 2019. Predicting humorousness and metaphor novelty with Gaussian process preference learning. In *Proceedings of the 57th Annual Meeting of the Association for Computational Linguistics*, pages 5716–5728, Florence, Italy. Association for Computational Linguistics.

Edwin Simpson and Iryna Gurevych. 2020. Scalable Bayesian preference learning for crowds. *Machine Learning*, pages 1–30.

Edwin D. Simpson and Iryna Gurevych. 2019. A Bayesian approach for sequence tagging with crowds. In *Proceedings of the 2019 Conference on Empirical Methods in Natural Language Processing and the 9th International Joint Conference on Natural Language Processing (EMNLP-IJCNLP)*, pages 1093–1104, Hong Kong, China. Association for Computational Linguistics.

Yan Yan, Rómer Rosales, Glenn Fung, Ramanathan Subramanian, and Jennifer Dy. 2014. Learning from multiple annotators with varying expertise. *Machine Learning*, 95(3):291–327.

Li'ang Yin, Jianhua Han, Weinan Zhang, and Yong Yu. 2017. Aggregating crowd wisdoms with label-aware autoencoders. In *Proceedings of the Twenty-Sixth International Joint Conference on Artificial Intelligence, IJCAI-17*, pages 1325–1331.

Yudian Zheng, Guoliang Li, Yuanbing Li, Caihua Shan, and Reynold Cheng. 2017. Truth inference in crowdsourcing: Is the problem solved? *Proc. VLDB Endow.*, 10(5):541–552.

Tutorial: End-to-End Speech Translation

Jan Niehues[1], Elizabeth Salesky[2], Marco Turchi[3] and Matteo Negri[3]
[1]Maastricht University
[2]Johns Hopkins University
[3]Fondazione Bruno Kessler
jan.niehues@maastrichtuniversity.nl esalesky@jhu.edu
{turchi,negri}@fbk.eu

Abstract

Speech translation is the translation of speech in one language typically to text in another, traditionally accomplished through a combination of automatic speech recognition and machine translation. Speech translation has attracted interest for many years, but the recent successful applications of deep learning to both individual tasks have enabled new opportunities through joint modeling, in what we today call 'end-to-end speech translation.'

In this tutorial we will introduce the techniques used in cutting-edge research on speech translation. Starting from the traditional cascaded approach, we will given an overview on data sources and model architectures to achieve state-of-the art performance with end-to-end speech translation for both high- and low-resource languages. In addition, we will discuss methods to evaluate analyze the proposed solutions, as well as the challenges faced when applying speech translation models for real-world applications.

1 Description

Machine translation (MT) and automatic speech recognition (ASR) have been mainstays of the speech and natural language processing communities for decades. Speech translation (ST), the combination of both tasks to translate from speech in one language typically to text in another, has existed for nearly as long as either of these (Waibel et al., 1991), attracting interest from both academia and industry. Until very recently, however, research in this area involved a cascade of separately trained speech recognition and machine translation models, with main questions pertaining to intermediate representations and processing steps to best connect these models.

The successful application of deep learning methods to speech and language processing has not only significantly improved the quality of models for both tasks (Sennrich et al., 2016; Hinton et al., 2012), but has also enabled new opportunities through joint modeling of speech and translation in what is today referred to as end-to-end speech translation (Bérard et al., 2016; Weiss et al., 2017). By integrating ideas from machine translation and speech recognition, this research topic is at the intersection of speech and language processing, traditionally two separate communities.

The paradigm switch to neural, end-to-end models has brought a significant increase in research interest and data resources for ST. The yearly evaluation campaign organized by IWSLT has seen large increases in participation in recent years (Ansari et al., 2020), and this year brought the creation of a joint special interest group (SIGSLT) spanning the ACL and ISCA communities. "Simpler" sequence-to-sequence architectures have lowered the barrier to entry; where previously researchers wishing to work in this area typically needed to either have significant knowledge of both ASR and MT or work in large collaborations, this is no longer the case. However, it remains the case that the best-performing models do draw on insights from both of these fields, and so we think that the time is ripe for a tutorial to better introduce the techniques to do cutting-edge research in ST.

This tutorial will summarize recent developments in end-to-end speech translation. We will start with discussion about the term 'end-to-end'[1] as well as a comparison to the traditional cascaded approach. In the subsequent sections, we will summarize ideas leveraged from automatic speech recognition (e.g. Chan et al. (2016)) and machine translation (e.g. Vaswani et al. (2017)) that are part of current state-of-the-art models, which are cur-

[1]For example, is use of pretrained models end-to-end? Is use of additional steps to create auxiliary target tasks like phoneme recognition? When do these distinctions matter?

Proceedings of EACL: Tutorials, pages 10–13
April 19 - 20, 2021.

rently demonstrated through evaluation campaigns like IWSLT. A particular focus point of the tutorial will be the current data landscape, as well as techniques to exploit different resources (Kano et al., 2020; Sperber et al., 2019) to enable speech translation not just for the few high-resource languages for which multi-parallel speech, transcripts, and translations exist.

After the survey of current state-of-the-art methods, we will present evaluation and analysis methods, and challenges when bringing these models from the lab to real-world environments. For example, one challenge of end-to-end models is their 'opaqueness'; with one joint system, it is more difficult to isolate causes of particular model behaviors and perhaps intervene, to avoid situations where key terms are translated in unexpected ways. Further, most training examples used fixed, pre-segmented input with parallel sentences, while in most practical applications the audio is not segmented. This brings additional challenges both in processing and also scoring. Finally, there are aspects of speech, such as speaker gender, accent, and prosody, which in cascaded systems the MT model did not have access to. We will touch on the impacts of some of these aspects, and provide greater detail about the specific example of gender bias mitigation (Bentivogli et al., 2020).

During the tutorial, we will highlight the present successes and challenges in end-to-end speech translation using examples from current state-of-the-art systems. Resources and teaching materials will be made available at `https://st-tutorial.github.io`.

2 Tutorial Type

This tutorial will cover cutting-edge research in the emerging field of end-to-end speech translation, and the aspects from speech and MT needed for this interdisciplinary research. The topic has not been previously covered in *CL tutorials.

3 Outline

- Introduction **(30 min)**
  - Task definition
  - Challenges/differences in translating speech rather than text
  - Traditional cascade approach to ST
- End-to-End **(45 min)**
  - Current state (high level overview)
  - Input representation
  - Architecture modifications
  - Output representation
- Data **(30 min)**
  - Available data for end-to-end ST
  - Different ways to leverage data sources:
    - Multi-task learning
    - Transfer learning and pretraining
    - Alternate data representations (e.g. phonemes)
- Evaluation/Analysis **(20 min)**
  - Automatic metrics
  - Utterance segmentation for automatic scoring
  - Mitigating errors due to speaker variation (gender, accent, etc.)
- Advanced topics **(30 min)**
  - Utterance segmentation
  - Making ST work for under-resourced languages
  - Multilingual ST
- From the lab to the real-world **(20 min)**
  - Automatic generation of subtitles
  - Simultaneous translation
  - Other Topics: system intervention, etc
- Conclusion **(5 min)**

4 Prerequisites

We would assume acquaintance with basic knowledge of machine learning and sequence-to-sequence models for machine translation, such as are covered in most introductory NLP courses. Any programming examples will be shown in Python.

5 Reading list

- Survey paper (Sperber and Paulik, 2020)
- The first papers on end-to-end ST (Bérard et al., 2016; Weiss et al., 2017)
- Data for end-to-end ST (Di Gangi et al., 2019b)
- Integrating additional data (Bansal et al., 2019; Jia et al., 2019; Sperber et al., 2019)

- Data representation (Salesky and Black, 2020)
- Adapting the Transformer for ST (Di Gangi et al., 2019a)
- Multilingual models (Inaguma et al., 2019)

6 Presenters

Jan Niehues, *Maastricht University*
Email: jan.niehues@maastrichtuniversity.nl
Website: `https://dke.maastrichtuniversity.nl/jan.niehues/`

Jan Niehues is an assistant professor at Maastricht University. He received his doctoral degree from Karlsruhe Institute of Technology in 2014 on the topic of "Domain Adaptation in Machine Translation." He has conducted research at Carnegie Mellon University and LIMSI/CNRS, Paris. His research has covered different aspects of Machine Translation and Spoken Language Translation. He has been involved in several international projects on spoken language translation e.g. the German-French Project Quaero, the H2020 EU project QT21 EU-Bridge and ELITR. Currently, he is one of the main organizers of the spoken language track in the IWSLT shared task.

Elizabeth Salesky, *Johns Hopkins University*
Email: esalesky@jhu.edu
Website: `https://esalesky.github.io`

Elizabeth Salesky is a PhD student at Johns Hopkins University. She has previously studied at Carnegie Mellon University, been a research assistant at Karlsruhe Institute of Technology, and worked at MIT Lincoln Laboratory, focused on speech and text translation. Her research focuses on speech translation for real-world and low-resource scenarios; e.g. phoneme features to reduce data dependence, disfluency removal in translating conversational speech, and learning robust representations. She has organized shared tasks on speech translation at IWSLT.

Marco Turchi, *Fondazione Bruno Kessler*
Email: turchi@fbk.eu
Website: `http://ict.fbk.eu/people/detail/marco-turchi/`

Marco Turchi is the head of the machine translation unit at Fondazione Bruno Kessler (FBK). He received his PhD degree in Computer Science from the U. of Siena, Italy in 2006. Before joining FBK in 2012, he worked at the European Commission, at the University of Bristol, at the Xerox Research Centre Europe, and at Yahoo Research Lab. His research activities focus on various aspects of sequence-to-sequence modelling applied to machine translation, speech translation and automatic post-editing. He is the co-organizer of the Conference of Machine Translation, the Spoken Language Translation Workshop and the automatic post-editing evaluation campaigns. He has been involved in several EU projects such as SMART, Matecat, ModernMT and QT21. He was the recipient of the Amazon AWS ML Research Awards on the topic of end-to-end spoken language translation in rich data conditions. He is the secretary of the ISCA SIGSLT interest group.

Matteo Negri *Fondazione Bruno Kessler*
Email: negri@fbk.eu
Website: `https://ict.fbk.eu/people/detail/matteo-negri`

Matteo Negri is a senior researcher in the Machine Translation unit at Fondazione Bruno Kessler. He received his degree in Philosophy of Language from the University of Turin, Italy in 2000. His research interests are in the field of computational linguistics, particularly machine translation, spoken language translation, textual entailment and question answering. He worked in several EU projects (QT21, CRACKER, MMT, MateCat, CoSyne, QALL-ME) and co-organised conferences, workshops and evaluation campaigns in NLP and MT-related areas (including the Conference on Machine Translation, the International Workshop on Spoken Language Translation and SemEval shared tasks). Together with Marco Turchi, he was the recipient of an Amazon AWS ML Research Award on "End-to-end Spoken Language Translation in Rich Data Conditions."

References

Ebrahim Ansari, Amittai Axelrod, Nguyen Bach, Ondřej Bojar, Roldano Cattoni, Fahim Dalvi, Nadir Durrani, Marcello Federico, Christian Federmann, Jiatao Gu, Fei Huang, Kevin Knight, Xutai Ma, Ajay Nagesh, Matteo Negri, Jan Niehues, Juan Pino, Elizabeth Salesky, Xing Shi, Sebastian Stüker, Marco Turchi, Alexander Waibel, and Changhan Wang. 2020. FINDINGS OF THE IWSLT 2020 EVALU-

ATION CAMPAIGN. In *Proceedings of the 17th International Conference on Spoken Language Translation*, pages 1–34, Online. Association for Computational Linguistics.

Sameer Bansal, Herman Kamper, Karen Livescu, Adam Lopez, and Sharon Goldwater. 2019. Pre-training on high-resource speech recognition improves low-resource speech-to-text translation. In *Proceedings of the 2019 Conference of the North American Chapter of the Association for Computational Linguistics: Human Language Technologies, Volume 1 (Long and Short Papers)*, pages 58–68, Minneapolis, Minnesota. Association for Computational Linguistics.

Luisa Bentivogli, Beatrice Savoldi, Matteo Negri, Mattia A. Di Gangi, Roldano Cattoni, and Marco Turchi. 2020. Gender in danger? evaluating speech translation technology on the MuST-SHE corpus. In *Proceedings of the 58th Annual Meeting of the Association for Computational Linguistics*, pages 6923–6933, Online. Association for Computational Linguistics.

Alexandre Bérard, Olivier Pietquin, Christophe Servan, and Laurent Besacier. 2016. Listen and Translate: A Proof of Concept for End-to-End Speech-to-Text Translation. In *NIPS Workshop on end-to-end learning for speech and audio processing*, Barcelona, Spain.

W. Chan, N. Jaitly, Q. Le, and O. Vinyals. 2016. Listen, attend and spell: A neural network for large vocabulary conversational speech recognition. In *2016 IEEE International Conference on Acoustics, Speech and Signal Processing (ICASSP)*, pages 4960–4964.

Mattia A Di Gangi, Matteo Negri, and Marco Turchi. 2019a. Adapting transformer to end-to-end spoken language translation. In *INTERSPEECH 2019*, pages 1133–1137. International Speech Communication Association (ISCA).

Mattia Antonino Di Gangi, Roldano Cattoni, Luisa Bentivogli, Matteo Negri, and Marco Turchi. 2019b. MuST-C: a Multilingual Speech Translation Corpus. In *Proceedings of the 2019 Conference of the North American Chapter of the Association for Computational Linguistics: Human Language Technologies (NAACL-HLT)*, page 2012–2017, Minneapolis, Minnesota.

G. Hinton, L. Deng, D. Yu, G. E. Dahl, A. Mohamed, N. Jaitly, A. Senior, V. Vanhoucke, P. Nguyen, T. N. Sainath, and B. Kingsbury. 2012. Deep neural networks for acoustic modeling in speech recognition: The shared views of four research groups. *IEEE Signal Processing Magazine*, 29(6):82–97.

Hirofumi Inaguma, Kevin Duh, Tatsuya Kawahara, and Shinji Watanabe. 2019. Multilingual end-to-end speech translation. In *2019 IEEE Automatic Speech Recognition and Understanding Workshop (ASRU)*, pages 570–577. IEEE.

Ye Jia, Melvin Johnson, Wolfgang Macherey, Ron J Weiss, Yuan Cao, Chung-Cheng Chiu, Naveen Ari, Stella Laurenzo, and Yonghui Wu. 2019. Leveraging weakly supervised data to improve end-to-end speech-to-text translation. In *ICASSP 2019-2019 IEEE International Conference on Acoustics, Speech and Signal Processing (ICASSP)*, pages 7180–7184. IEEE.

T. Kano, S. Sakti, and S. Nakamura. 2020. End-to-end speech translation with transcoding by multi-task learning for distant language pairs. *IEEE/ACM Transactions on Audio, Speech, and Language Processing*, 28:1342–1355.

Elizabeth Salesky and Alan W Black. 2020. Phone features improve speech translation. In *Proceedings of the 58th Annual Meeting of the Association for Computational Linguistics*, pages 2388–2397, Online. Association for Computational Linguistics.

Rico Sennrich, Barry Haddow, and Alexandra Birch. 2016. Edinburgh neural machine translation systems for wmt 16. In *Proceedings of the First Conference on Machine Translation*, pages 371–376, Berlin, Germany. Association for Computational Linguistics.

Matthias Sperber, Graham Neubig, Jan Niehues, and Alex Waibel. 2019. Attention-Passing Models for Robust and Data-Efficient End-to-End Speech Translation. *Transactions of the Association for Computational Linguistics (TACL)*.

Matthias Sperber and Matthias Paulik. 2020. Speech Translation and the End-to-End Promise: Taking Stock of Where We Are. In *Association for Computational Linguistic (ACL)*, Seattle, USA.

Ashish Vaswani, Noam Shazeer, Niki Parmar, Jakob Uszkoreit, Llion Jones, Aidan N. Gomez, undefinedukasz Kaiser, and Illia Polosukhin. 2017. Attention is all you need. In *Proceedings of the 31st International Conference on Neural Information Processing Systems*, NIPS'17, page 6000–6010, Red Hook, NY, USA. Curran Associates Inc.

A. Waibel, A. N. Jain, A. E. McNair, H. Saito, A. G. Hauptmann, and J. Tebelskis. 1991. Janus: A speech-to-speech translation system using connectionist and symbolic processing strategies. In *Proceedings of the Acoustics, Speech, and Signal Processing, 1991. ICASSP-91., 1991 International Conference*, ICASSP '91, page 793–796, USA. IEEE Computer Society.

Ron J Weiss, Jan Chorowski, Navdeep Jaitly, Yonghui Wu, and Zhifeng Chen. 2017. Sequence-to-sequence models can directly translate foreign speech. *Proc. Interspeech 2017*, pages 2625–2629.

Reviewing Natural Language Processing Research

Kevin B. Cohen
Computational Bioscience Program
University of Colorado, USA
kevin.cohen@gmail.com

Karën Fort
Sorbonne Université, EA STIH, Paris
LORIA, Nancy
France
karen.fort@sorbonne-universite.fr

Margot Mieskes
University of Applied Sciences, Darmstadt
Germany
margot.mieskes@h-da.de

Aurélie Névéol
LIMSI, CNRS
Université Paris-Saclay
France
neveol@limsi.fr

Anna Rogers
University of Copenhagen, Copenhagen
Denmark
anna.gld@gmail.com

Abstract

The reviewing procedure has been identified as one of the major issues in the current situation of the NLP field. While it is implicitly assumed that junior researcher learn reviewing during their PhD project, this might not always be the case. Additionally, with the growing NLP community and the efforts in the context of widening the NLP community, researchers joining the field might not have the opportunity to practise reviewing. This tutorial fills in this gap by providing an opportunity to learn the basics of reviewing. Also more experienced researchers might find this tutorial interesting to revise their reviewing procedure.

1 Tutorial Content

This tutorial will cover the theory and practice of reviewing research in natural language processing. As has been pointed out for years by leading figures in our community (Webber, 2007), researchers in the ACL community face a heavy—and growing—reviewing burden. Initiatives to lower this burden have been discussed at the recent ACL general assembly in Florence (ACL 2019)[1]. Simultaneously, notable "false negatives"—rejection by our conferences of work that was later shown to be tremendously important after acceptance by *other* conferences (Church, 2005)—have raised awareness of the fact that our reviewing practices leave something to be desired... and we do not often talk about "false positives" with respect to conference papers, but conversations in the hallways at *ACL meetings suggest that we have a publication bias towards papers that report high performance, with perhaps not much else of interest in them (Manning, 2015).

It need not be this way. Reviewing is a learnable skill (Basford, 1990; Paice, 2001; Benos et al., 2003; Koike et al., 2009; Shukla, 2010; Tandon, 2014; Spyns and Vidal, 2015; Stahel and Moore, 2016; Kohnen, 2017; McFadden et al., 2017; Hill, 2018), and you will learn it here via a combination of lectures and a significant amount of hands-on practice.

Type: Introductory
Structure: see Table 1
Prerequisites: Proficiency in English

Table 1 presents a brief outline of the tutorial. Our aim is to provide enough options for hands-on experience and smaller-group activities in breakout rooms.

1.1 Reading List

- Kenneth Church. 2005. Last words: Reviewing the reviewers. *Computational Linguistics*, 31(4):575–578
- Button K. S., Bal L., Clark A., and Shipley T. 2016. Preventing the ends from justifying the means: withholding results to address publication bias in peer-review. *BMC Psychol.*, 4(1)
- Leif Engqvist and Joachim Frommen. 2008. Double-blind peer review and gender publication bias. *Animal Behaviour*, 76:e1–e2

[1] http://www.livecongress.it/aol/indexSA.php?id=E2EAED7D&ticket=

Proceedings of EACL: Tutorials, pages 14–16
April 19 - 20, 2021. ©2020 Association for Computational Linguistics

Slot	Content
1	Role of peer review in scientific publishing
2	General Procedure in Reviewing – Overview on Various Review Forms & Best Practise
3	Approaches to reviewing and NLP-specific issues
4	Section-specific criteria (Materials & Methods, Results, etc.)
5	Ethics of reviewing
6	How to give kind, constructive, and helpful feedback efficiently
7	Wrap-Up

Table 1: Rough outline of the planned schedule, which will be accommodated according to audience expertise and input. Each slot will also include practical exercises in smaller groups.

- Michael J. Mahoney. 1977. Publication prejudices: An experimental study of confirmatory bias in the peer review system. *Cognitive Therapy and Research*, 1(2):161–175
- Mark Steedman. 2008. Last words: On becoming a discipline. *Computational Linguistics*, 34(1):137–144
- Bonnie Webber. 2007. Breaking news: Changing attitudes and practices. *Computational Linguistics*, 33(4):607–611

1.2 Presenters (in alphabetical order)

Kevin Bretonnel Cohen has written, overseen, and received hundreds of reviews in his capacity as deputy editor-in-chief of a biomedical informatics journal, associate editor of five natural language processing or bioinformatics journals, special issue editor, workshop organizer, and author of 100+ publications in computational linguistics and natural language processing. His forthcoming book *Writing about data science research: With examples from machine and natural language processing* includes coverage of a number of aspects of the reviewing process. His current research focuses on issues of reproducibility.

Karën Fort is an associate professor at Sorbonne Université. Besides being a reviewer for most major NLP conferences, she has been editor in chief for a *Traitement automatique des langues* journal special issue on ethics and acted as Area Chair for ACL in 2017 and 2018 (as senior AC). She co-authored the report on the EMNLP reviewer survey (Névéol et al., 2017).

Margot Mieskes is a professor at the Darmstadt University of Applied Sciences. She has written and received reviews for numerous conferences and journals. She is a member of the ACL Professional Conduct Committee and an active member of the Widening NLP efforts. She co-authored the report on EMNLP reviewer survey (Névéol et al., 2017).

Aurélie Névéol is a permanent researcher at LIMSI CNRS and Université Paris Saclay. She has been involved in reviewing natural language processing papers at many stages of the reviewing process, including: reviewer, associate editor for three journals, area chair for *ACL and bioinformatics conferences, workshop organizer. Her research focuses on biomedical natural language processing as well as ethics issues in NLP research. She co-authored the report on EMNLP reviewer survey (Névéol et al., 2017).

Anna Rogers is a post-doctoral associate at the University of Copenhagen. Her main research areas are interpretability, evaluation and analysis of deep learning models for NLP. She is also active in the sphere of meta-research and methodology, working on issues in peer review and organizing the Workshop on Insights from Negative Results in NLP (EMNLP 2020, 2021).

References

P Basford. 1990. How to... review an article. *Nursing times*, 86(40):61–61.

Dale J Benos, Kevin L Kirk, and John E Hall. 2003. How to review a paper. *Advances in physiology education*, 27(2):47–52.

Kenneth Church. 2005. Last words: Reviewing the reviewers. *Computational Linguistics*, 31(4):575–578.

Leif Engqvist and Joachim Frommen. 2008. Double-blind peer review and gender publication bias. *Animal Behaviour*, 76:e1–e2.

Michael D Hill. 2018. How to review a clinical research paper. *Stroke*, 49(5):e204–e206.

Thomas Kohnen. 2017. How to write a good peer review. *Journal of Cataract & Refractive Surgery*, 43(10):1243–1244.

Kaoru Koike, Luca Ansaloni, Fausto Catena, and Ernest E Moore. 2009. WJES: how to review a clinical paper. *World Journal of Emergency Surgery*, 4(1):8.

Michael J. Mahoney. 1977. Publication prejudices: An experimental study of confirmatory bias in the peer review system. *Cognitive Therapy and Research*, 1(2):161–175.

Christopher D Manning. 2015. Computational linguistics and deep learning. *Computational Linguistics*, 41(4):701–707.

David McFadden, Scott LeMaire, Michael Sarr, and Kevin Behrns. 2017. How to review a paper: Suggestions from the editors of surgery and the journal of surgical research. *Surgery*, 162(1):1–6.

Aurélie Névéol, Karën Fort, and Rebecca Hwa. 2017. Report on EMNLP Reviewer Survey. Technical report, Association for Computational Linguistics.

Elisabeth Paice. 2001. How to write a peer review. *Hospital Medicine*, 62(3):172–175.

Button K. S., Bal L., Clark A., and Shipley T. 2016. Preventing the ends from justifying the means: withholding results to address publication bias in peer-review. *BMC Psychol.*, 4(1).

Satish K Shukla. 2010. How to review an article. *Indian Journal of Surgery*, 72(2):93–96.

Peter Spyns and María-Esther Vidal. 2015. *Scientific Peer Reviewing: Practical Hints and Best Practices*. Springer.

Philip F Stahel and Ernest E Moore. 2016. How to review a surgical paper: a guide for junior referees. *BMC medicine*, 14(1):29.

Mark Steedman. 2008. Last words: On becoming a discipline. *Computational Linguistics*, 34(1):137–144.

Rajiv Tandon. 2014. How to review a scientific paper. *Asian journal of psychiatry*, 11:124–127.

Bonnie Webber. 2007. Breaking news: Changing attitudes and practices. *Computational Linguistics*, 33(4):607–611.

Advances and Challenges in Unsupervised Neural Machine Translation

Rui Wang and Hai Zhao
Department of Computer Science and Engineering, Shanghai Jiao Tong University
Key Laboratory of Shanghai Education Commission for Intelligent Interaction and Cognitive Engineering, Shanghai Jiao Tong University, Shanghai, China
MoE Key Lab of Artificial Intelligence, AI Institute,
Shanghai Jiao Tong University, Shanghai, China
wangrui.nlp@gmail.com and zhaohai@cs.sjtu.edu.cn

Abstract

Unsupervised cross-lingual language representation initialization methods, together with mechanisms such as denoising and back-translation, have advanced unsupervised neural machine translation (UNMT), which has achieved impressive results. Meanwhile, there are still several challenges for UNMT. This tutorial first introduces the background and the latest progress of UNMT. We then examine a number of challenges to UNMT and give empirical results on how well the technology currently holds up[1].

1 Tutorial Content

1.1 Introduction

Machine translation (MT) is a classic topic in the NLP community. Since 2010s, deep learning methods have been adopted in neural MT (NMT) and NMT has achieved promising performances (Bahdanau et al., 2015). Recently, NMT has been adapted to the unsupervised scenario. Unsupervised NMT (UNMT) (Artetxe et al., 2018b; Lample et al., 2018a) only requires monolingual corpora, using a combination of diverse mechanisms such as an initialization with bilingual word embeddings, denoising auto-encoder, back-translation, and shared latent representation.

1.2 Methods

Cross-lingual language representation initialization. In supervised NMT, language representation initialization is not so necessary, because the bilingual corpus can help NMT learn the cross-lingual representation. In comparison, there is only monolingual corpus for UNMT. Therefore, the pre-trained unsupervised bilingual word embedding (Artetxe et al., 2017; Lample et al., 2018b) or unsupervised cross-lingual language model (Lample and Conneau, 2019) provide a naive translation knowledge to enable the back-translation to generate pseudo-parallel corpora at the beginning of the UNMT training.

Denoising auto-encoder: Noise obtained by randomly performing local substitutions and word reorderings (Vincent et al., 2010), is added to the input sentences to improve model learning ability and regularization. The denoising auto-encoder model objective function would be optimized by maximizing the probability of encoding a *noisy* sentence and reconstructing it.

Back-translation: The back-translation plays a key role in achieving unsupervised translation relying only on monolingual corpora in each language (Sennrich et al., 2016). The pseudo-parallel sentence pairs produced by the model at the previous iteration have been used to train the new translation model.

Sharing latent representations: Encoders and decoders are (partially) shared for two languages. Therefore, the two languages must use the same vocabulary. The entire training of UNMT needs to consider back-translation between the two languages and their respective denoising processing.

1.3 Recent Advances

USMT and UNMT. Since 2016, statistical MT (SMT) has been significantly over-passed by NMT. Lample et al. (2018c) and Artetxe et al. (2018a) proposed an alternative method, that is, unsupervised statistical machine translation (USMT) method. However, in the supervised scenario, the performance of USMT method is comparable with that of UNMT. In addition, several works (Marie and Fujita, 2018; Ren et al., 2019; Artetxe et al., 2019) combined UNMT and USMT to improve unsupervised machine translation performance. In WMT-

[1] https://wangruinlp.github.io/unmt.html

Proceedings of EACL: Tutorials, pages 17–21
April 19 - 20, 2021. ©2020 Association for Computational Linguistics

2019, the unsupervised MT task (German-Czech) first-time became the officially task of WMT, and the system from NICT (Marie et al., 2019) won the first place and achieved state-of-the-art performances by combining the USMT and UNMT. However, after the advanced pre-training technologies was developed, USMT became less important.

Advanced Pre-Training Technologies. Similar as other NLP tasks, the quality of language representation pre-training significantly affects the performance of UNMT. Several works focus on improving the language representation pre-training. Sun et al. (2019b) proposed to train UNMT jointly with bilingual word embedding agreement. More recently, it has been shown that the pre-trained cross-lingual language model (Lample and Conneau, 2019; Song et al., 2019) achieve better UNMT performance than the bilingual word embedding. In high-resource scenario, UNMT has achieved remarkable performance. However, the performance of low-resource UNMT is still far below expectations

Multilingualism. To improve the low-resource UNMT, multi-lingual UNMT (MUNMT) is proposed (Sun et al., 2020; Liu et al., 2020). The translation of low-resouce and zero-shot language pairs can be enhanced by the similar languages in the shared latent representation. In addition, the pivot-based methods are proposed. Leng et al. (2019) introduced unsupervised pivot translation for distant language pairs. The SJTU-NICT team used monolingual corpus together with parallel third-party languages to enhance the low-resource UNMT performance (Li et al., 2020b) and their system achieved the best performance in WMT-2020 unsupervised task (Li et al., 2020a).

1.4 Challenges

Most existing works focus on modeling UNMT systems and few works investigate the reason why UNMT works and the scenario where UNMT works. UNMT still has limit performance in the distant language pair and domain-specific scenarios.

Distant Language Pairs. we will first empirically show that the performances of UNMT in distant language pairs (Chinese/Japanese-English) are much worse than the similar language pairs (German/French-English). Then, we will show the hypotheses: 1) syntactic structures of distant language pairs are quit different. Without parallel supervision, it is very difficult for UNMT to learn the syntactic correspondence. 2) There are too few shared words/subwords in the distant language pair to learn the shared latent representation for UNMT. Finally, we will show some potential solutions, such as 1) syntactic methods (Eriguchi et al., 2016; Chen et al., 2017, 2018) and 2) artificial shared words/code-switching methods (Yang et al., 2020) and show the initial results.

Domain adaptation methods for UNMT have not been well-studied although UNMT has recently achieved remarkable results in some specific domains for several language pairs. For UNMT, addition to inconsistent domains between training data and test data for supervised NMT, there also exist other inconsistent domains between monolingual training data in two languages. Actually, it is difficult for some language pairs to obtain enough source and target monolingual corpora from the same domain in the real-world scenario.

In this tutorial, we will empirically show different scenarios for unsupervised domain-specific neural machine translation. Based on these scenarios, we will show and analyze several potential solutions including batch weighting, data selection, and fine tuning methods, to improve the performances of domain-specific UNMT systems (Sun et al., 2019a).

Efficiency. Compared with NMT, the training time of UNMT increased rapidly. In addition, learning sharing latent representations ties the performance of both translation directions, especially for distant language pairs, while denoising dramatically delays convergence by continuously modifying the training data. Efficient training of UNMT is also an issue that needs to be solved.

2 Relevance to the Computational Linguistics Community

This tutorial makes an attempt to review the latest progress on UNMT by introducing advances and challenges for UNMT. MT is a classic topic in the NLP community. Recently, UNMT has attracted great interest in the researchers in both the MT/NLP community and industry.

This tutorial is primarily towards researchers who have a basic understanding of deep learning based NLP. We believe that this tutorial would help the audience more deeply understand UNMT.

Presenter: Rui Wang		Presenter: Hai Zhao	
1. Introduction of MT (30 min)	2. Methods for UNMT (70 min)	3. Challenges in UNMT (60 min)	4. Summary (20 min)
1.1 Statistical MT (SMT)	2.1 USMT and UNMT	3.1 Distant Language Pairs	4.1 Conclusion
1.2 Neural MT (NMT)	2.2 Advanced Pre-Training Technologies	3.2 Domain Adaptation	4.2 Future Trends
	2.3 Multilingualism	3.3 Training Efficiency	
– Coffee Break – (30 min)			

Table 1: Tutorial outlines

3 Type of the Tutorial: Cutting-edge

We introduce the cutting-edge technologies. This tutorial is primarily towards researchers who have a basic understanding of deep learning based NLP, and it is supposed to widen and deepen the understanding of cutting-edge NLP for the audience.

4 Tutorial Outlines

We will present our tutorial in three hours. The detailed tutorial outlines are shown in Table 1.

5 Specification of Any Prerequisites for the Attendees

This tutorial is primarily aimed at researchers who have a basic understanding of NLP and deep learning.

6 Small reading list

- Neural Machine Translation: the basic method "*Neural machine translation by jointly learning to align and translate*" (Bahdanau et al., 2015) and the related deep learning backgrounds "*Deep learning*" (LeCun et al., 2015).
- UNMT: the basic methods "*Unsupervised neural machine translation*" (Artetxe et al., 2018b) and "*Unsupervised machine translation using monolingual corpora only*" (Lample et al., 2018a). State-of-the-art UNMT systems (Marie et al., 2019; Li et al., 2020a).

7 Presenters

1. Dr. Rui Wang, Associate Professor, Department of Computer Science and Engineering, Shanghai Jiao Tong University, China.
wangrui.nlp@gmail.com
https://wangruinlp.github.io

His research focuses on machine translation (MT), a classic task in NLP. His recent interests are traditional linguistic based and cutting-edge machine learning based approaches for MT. He (as the first or the corresponding authors) has published more than 40 MT papers in top-tier NLP/ML/AI conferences and journals, such as ACL, EMNLP, ICLR, AAAI, IJCAI, TPAMI, TASLP, etc. He has also won several first places in top-tier MT shared tasks, such as WMT-2018, WMT-2019, WMT-2020, etc.

He has given several tutorials, such as EACL-2021, EMNLP-2021, CCMT-2019, etc. He served as the area chairs of ICLR-2021 and NAACL-2021.

2. Dr. Hai Zhao, Professor, Department of Computer Science and Engineering, Shanghai Jiao Tong University, China.
zhaohai@cs.sjtu.edu.cn
http://bcmi.sjtu.edu.cn/~zhaohai

His research interest is natural language processing. He has published more than 120 papers in ACL, EMNLP, COLING, ICLR, AAAI, IJCAI, and IEEE TPAMI/TKDE/TASLP. He won the first places in several NLP shared tasks, such as CoNLL and SIGHAN Bakeoff and top ranking in remarkable machine reading comprehension task leaderboards such as SQuAD2.0 and RACE.

He has taught the course "natural language processing" in SJTU for more than 10 years. He has given several tutorials, such as EACL-2021, EMNLP-2021, etc. He is ACL-2017 area chair on parsing, and ACL-2018/2019 (senior) area chairs on morphology and word segmentation.

References

Mikel Artetxe, Gorka Labaka, and Eneko Agirre. 2017. Learning bilingual word embeddings with (almost) no bilingual data. In *Proceedings of the 55th Annual*

Meeting of the Association for Computational Linguistics (Volume 1: Long Papers), pages 451–462, Vancouver, Canada.

Mikel Artetxe, Gorka Labaka, and Eneko Agirre. 2018a. Unsupervised statistical machine translation. In *Proceedings of the 2018 Conference on Empirical Methods in Natural Language Processing*, pages 3632–3642, Brussels, Belgium.

Mikel Artetxe, Gorka Labaka, and Eneko Agirre. 2019. An effective approach to unsupervised machine translation. In *Proceedings of the 57th Annual Meeting of the Association for Computational Linguistics*, pages 194–203, Florence, Italy.

Mikel Artetxe, Gorka Labaka, Eneko Agirre, and Kyunghyun Cho. 2018b. Unsupervised neural machine translation. In *Proceedings of the Sixth International Conference on Learning Representations*, Vancouver, Canada.

Dzmitry Bahdanau, Kyunghyun Cho, and Yoshua Bengio. 2015. Neural machine translation by jointly learning to align and translate. In *International Conference on Learning Representations*, San Diego, CA.

Kehai Chen, Rui Wang, Masao Utiyama, Lemao Liu, Akihiro Tamura, Eiichiro Sumita, and Tiejun Zhao. 2017. Neural machine translation with source dependency representation. In *Proceedings of the 2017 Conference on Empirical Methods in Natural Language Processing*, pages 2846–2852, Copenhagen, Denmark.

Kehai Chen, Rui Wang, Masao Utiyama, Eiichiro Sumita, and Tiejun Zhao. 2018. Syntax-directed attention for neural machine translation. In *Proceedings of the AAAI Conference on Artificial Intelligence*, pages 4792–4799, New Olreans, LA.

Akiko Eriguchi, Kazuma Hashimoto, and Yoshimasa Tsuruoka. 2016. Tree-to-sequence attentional neural machine translation. In *Proceedings of the 54th Annual Meeting of the Association for Computational Linguistics (Volume 1: Long Papers)*, pages 823–833, Berlin, Germany.

Guillaume Lample and Alexis Conneau. 2019. Cross-lingual language model pretraining. In *Advances in Neural Information Processing Systems*, Vancouver, Canada.

Guillaume Lample, Alexis Conneau, Ludovic Denoyer, and Marc'Aurelio Ranzato. 2018a. Unsupervised machine translation using monolingual corpora only. In *Proceedings of the Sixth International Conference on Learning Representations*, Vancouver, Canada.

Guillaume Lample, Alexis Conneau, Marc'Aurelio Ranzato, Ludovic Denoyer, and Hervé Jégou. 2018b. Word translation without parallel data. In *International Conference on Learning Representations*, Vancouver, Canada.

Guillaume Lample, Myle Ott, Alexis Conneau, Ludovic Denoyer, and Marc'Aurelio Ranzato. 2018c. Phrase-based & neural unsupervised machine translation. In *Proceedings of the 2018 Conference on Empirical Methods in Natural Language Processing*, pages 5039–5049, Brussels, Belgium.

Yann LeCun, Yoshua Bengio, and Geoffrey Hinton. 2015. Deep learning. *nature*, 521(7553):436.

Yichong Leng, Xu Tan, Tao Qin, Xiang-Yang Li, and Tie-Yan Liu. 2019. Unsupervised pivot translation for distant languages. In *Proceedings of the 57th Annual Meeting of the Association for Computational Linguistics*, pages 175–183, Florence, Italy.

Zuchao Li, Hai Zhao, Rui Wang, Kehai Chen, Masao Utiyama, and Eiichiro Sumita. 2020a. SJTU-NICT's supervised and unsupervised neural machine translation systems for the WMT20 news translation task. *arXiv preprint arXiv:2010.05122*.

Zuchao Li, Hai Zhao, Rui Wang, Masao Utiyama, and Eiichiro Sumita. 2020b. Reference language based unsupervised neural machine translation. In *The 2020 Conference on Empirical Methods in Natural Language Processing: ACL Findings*.

Yinhan Liu, Jiatao Gu, Naman Goyal, Xian Li, Sergey Edunov, Marjan Ghazvininejad, Mike Lewis, and Luke Zettlemoyer. 2020. Multilingual denoising pre-training for neural machine translation.

Benjamin Marie and Atsushi Fujita. 2018. Unsupervised neural machine translation initialized by unsupervised statistical machine translation. *CoRR*, abs/1810.12703.

Benjamin Marie, Haipeng Sun, Rui Wang, Kehai Chen, Atsushi Fujita, Masao Utiyama, and Eiichiro Sumita. 2019. NICT's unsupervised neural and statistical machine translation systems for the WMT19 news translation task. In *Proceedings of the Fourth Conference on Machine Translation (Volume 2: Shared Task Papers, Day 1)*, pages 294–301, Florence, Italy. Association for Computational Linguistics.

Shuo Ren, Zhirui Zhang, Shujie Liu, Ming Zhou, and Shuai Ma. 2019. Unsupervised neural machine translation with SMT as posterior regularization. In *The Thirty-Third AAAI Conference on Artificial Intelligence*, pages 241–248, Honolulu, Hawaii, USA.

Rico Sennrich, Barry Haddow, and Alexandra Birch. 2016. Improving neural machine translation models with monolingual data. In *Proceedings of the 54th Annual Meeting of the Association for Computational Linguistics (Volume 1: Long Papers)*, pages 86–96, Berlin, Germany.

Kaitao Song, Xu Tan, Tao Qin, Jianfeng Lu, and Tie-Yan Liu. 2019. MASS: masked sequence to sequence pre-training for language generation. In *Proceedings of the 36th International Conference on Machine Learning*, pages 5926–5936, Long Beach, California, USA.

Haipeng Sun, Rui Wang, Kehai Chen, Masao Utiyama, Eiichiro Sumita, and Tiejun Zhao. 2019a. An empirical study of domain adaptation for unsupervised neural machine translation. *CoRR*, abs/1908.09605.

Haipeng Sun, Rui Wang, Kehai Chen, Masao Utiyama, Eiichiro Sumita, and Tiejun Zhao. 2019b. Unsupervised bilingual word embedding agreement for unsupervised neural machine translation. In *ACL*, pages 1235–1245, Florence, Italy.

Haipeng Sun, Rui Wang, Kehai Chen, Masao Utiyama, Eiichiro Sumita, and Tiejun Zhao. 2020. Knowledge distillation for multilingual unsupervised neural machine translation. In *Proceedings of the 58th Annual Meeting of the Association for Computational Linguistics*, pages 3525–3535, Online.

Pascal Vincent, Hugo Larochelle, Isabelle Lajoie, Yoshua Bengio, and Pierre-Antoine Manzagol. 2010. Stacked denoising autoencoders: Learning useful representations in a deep network with a local denoising criterion. *Journal of Machine Learning Research*, 11:3371–3408.

Zhen Yang, Bojie Hu, Ambyera Han, Shen Huang, and Qi Ju. 2020. Code-switching pre-training for neural machine translation. *arXiv: 2009.08088*.

Association for Computational Linguistics
209 N. Eighth Street
Stroudsburg, Pennsylvania 18360

ISBN 978-1-7138-2917-1

CURRAN ASSOCIATES INC.
proceedings.com